I VOTED

Voices of Tomorrow Starts with a Vote Today

By Letina Brady Pettis

Published By: Pen Legacy®

Library of Congress Cataloging – in- Publication Data has been applied for.
ISBN: 979-8-9918247-9-8
PRINTED IN THE UNITED STATES OF AMERICA.

AUTHOR'S NOTE:

I Voted was written to inspire future leaders on the power of their voices by voting and making a difference for future generations. Your understanding and action on this message is of utmost importance. I want youth readers to know, "Voting is an investment; your voice is your generational wealth."
Letina Brady Pettis

DEDICATION:

This book is dedicated to my grandchildren, to inspire them to continue the legacy of their great-grandfather and me, their grandmother, to exercise their right to vote and always make sure their voices are heard. And remember, "Voices of Tomorrow Starts With a Vote Today."
Letina Brady Pettis

As Tricee entered her teenage years, she became even more passionate about voting rights and getting her classmates involved in their community.

At school, Tricee joined the student council and quickly became a leader, organizing activities that got everyone involved in making a difference.

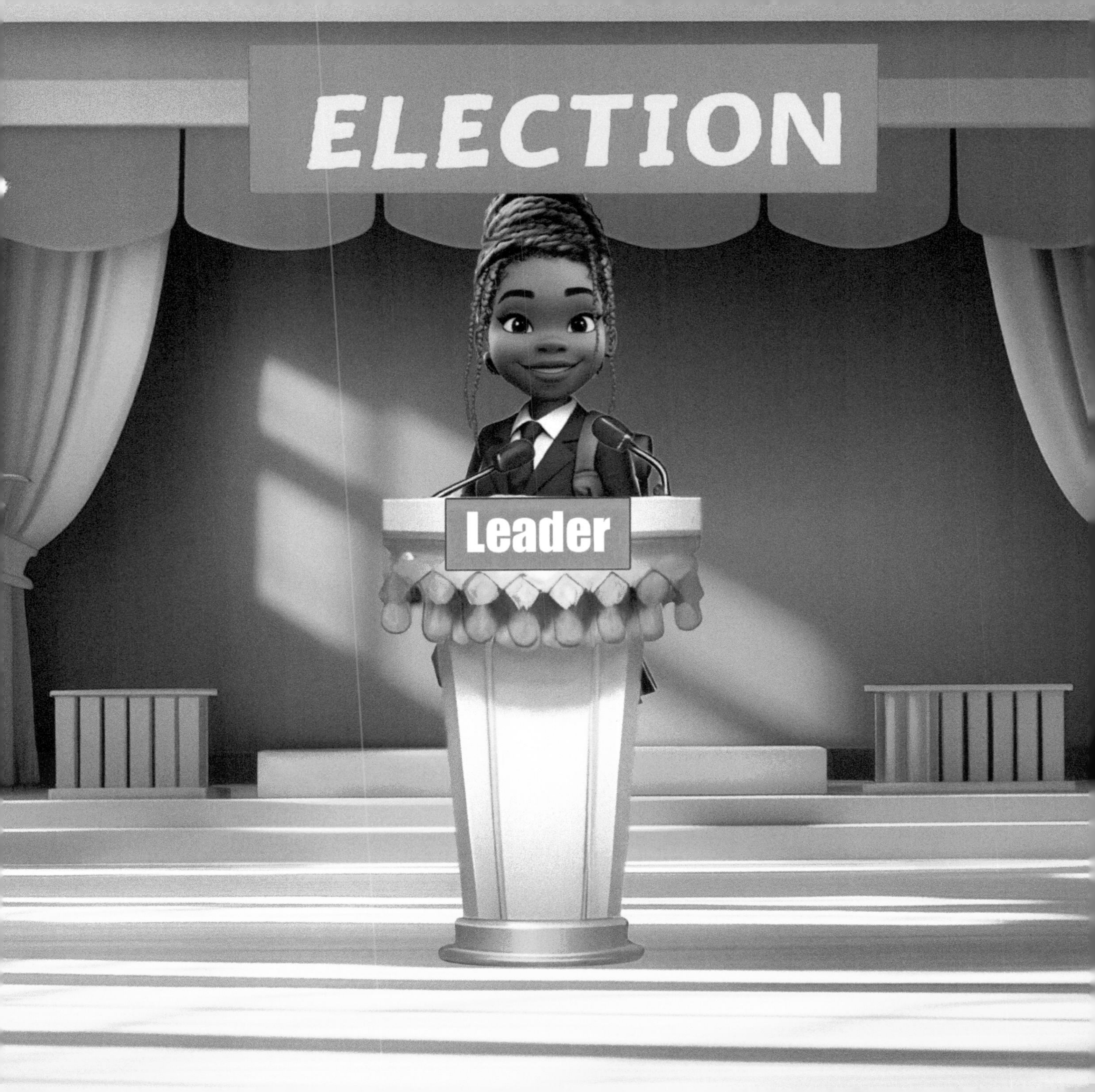
ELECTION
Leader

Tricee spoke at town hall meetings, encouraging teens to discuss issues that mattered to them and letting them know that their future begins with a vote today.

One day, Tricee heard her classmates talking about an upcoming election. Their excitement lit a spark in her.

"I want to vote!" Tricee thought, but she knew she wasn't old enough yet. So, she became a Deputy Registrar to help other teens register to vote and make sure their voices were heard.

Tricee also volunteered as an election judge to learn how voting worked at the local polling station.

Working at the polling station helped Tricee see how important every vote is.

Feeling motivated, Tricee created "Get Out the Vote (GOTV) 4 Teens" to help other young people get involved in voting.

She also founded National Teens Voter Registration Day, inspiring teens to register to vote and recognize their role in shaping the future.

Finally, on her eighteenth birthday, Tricee voted for the first time as her dad watched proudly. "I voted!" she exclaimed, feeling proud and knowing her vote and voice made a difference.

Tricee realized that her journey was not just for herself but also to guide and support others. She was determined to advocate for voter registration and civic engagement among her peers.

She volunteered at high schools, sharing her story and encouraging others to take their first steps toward voting.

Tricee's commitment and efforts inspired hope and optimism among her peers, showing them that their voices and votes matter.

Letina (Tina) Brady Pettis, a native of Chicago's south side, grew up inspired by the community leadership of her father and family members who advocated for voting rights —their role in shaping community perspectives instilled in Tina a deep commitment to public service.

Tina founded Get Out the Vote (GOTV) 4 Teens and National Teens Voter Registration Day. She is also the author of "I Want To Vote." Tina organizes voter registration drives throughout Chicago and its suburbs, which are dedicated to civic engagement and community building.

As the Director and Co-Chair of the League of Women Voters of Illinois-Issues and Advocacy and the Director-Issues and Advocacy for the League of Women Voters of Chicago, Tina has been instrumental in her advocacy extending to various community-focused groups, including Diversity and Inclusion and Community Oversight of Police, and the League of Women Voters of Cook County Criminal Justice Interest Group. She advocates for women's rights, the fight against gun violence, and voting rights.

Tina is an active member of several organizations, including The Links, Incorporated, the National Council of Negro Women, the National Coalition of 100 Black Women, and the National Women Veterans United. Her involvement in these groups further amplifies her commitment to social justice and community development.

In recognition of her dedication to community service, Tina has received the President of the United States Volunteer Service Award, the National Association of University Women-North Central Section Woman of the Year Award, the Top Ladies of Distinction Dorothy J. Fisher Community Service Servant Leader Award, the National Council of Negro Women-Chicago Midwest Section Women Making History Award, Chicago Defender Woman of Excellence Award, She Rocks It Award and the Zeta Pi Chapter of the Iota Phi Lambda Sorority, Incorporated, Leadership Award.

9 798991 824798